SUCCESS VITAMINS FOR A POSITIVE MIND

SUCCESS VITAMINS FOR A POSITIVE MIND

(Over 700 Mind Conditioners)
by Dr. Napoleon Hill

by Napoleon Hill
and Judith Williamson

An Approved Publication of The Napoleon Hill Foundation

MEDIA

Published 2019 by Gildan Media LLC
aka G&D Media
www.GandDmedia.com

Front Cover design by David Rheinhardt of Pyrographx

Interior design by Meghan Day Healey of Story Horse, LLC

Library of Congress Cataloging-in-Publication Data is available upon request

ISBN: 978-1-7225-0116-7

10   9   8   7   6   5   4   3   2   1

Introduction

Dr. Napoleon Hill is an expert in taking theory and resizing it into applicable practice for the layman. He is able to distill thought into short epigrams that he himself has labeled "Success Vitamins" for a daily dose of insight into how to succeed in today's complicated world. For businessmen and businesswomen alike who are watching their clocks but still need daily inspiration, this volume of over 700 success proverbs is ideal.

By just reading and reflecting on a few epigrams or even a page a day, you will be conditioning your mind for positive outcomes. These "Success Vitamins" can contribute to your healing financially, mentally, physically, spiritually, socially, and emotionally today and throughout the year. Topics are random, but the messages are always pertinent to concerns of your life—especially on the job. When thoughts are directed toward positive outcomes, positive behaviors follow.

Today's students of self-help accept the value of affirmations. Sometimes these short saying are called auto-suggestions and even self-hypnosis, but regardless of the name the result is that when read or repeated out loud with enthusiasm they work to modify behavior. These "Success Vitamins" can supply the missing ingredient that conditions a person for success—one short saying at a time. Each saying is a "truism" that expresses an idea that sometimes has been overlooked, forgotten, or covered up for the sake of convenience. When you read these, you will detect the eternal wisdom of the sayings.

The preface by Dr. Hill is well worth your study time too. In his typical style, he gets to the heart of the issue by stating that harmony is what is important and needed most now in both our inner and outer worlds. He compares this to the harmony Infinite Intelligence has placed in the universal workings of Cosmic Habitforce from the beginning of time. It is interesting to note that Dr. Hill finds harmony lacking only in mankind and he reminds us that it is better to mirror the flow of the universe than to oppose it for any and all of our purposes. The advice is as sound today as it was when he wrote his findings decades ago.

In using and applying this material, you will alter the blueprint of your life for the better. By just considering the ideas Dr. Hill crystallizes in these success epigrams, you will be attending a school for mind conditioning. Recalling that we get what we focus on, paying attention to these tidbits of wisdom aptly called "Success Vitamins" you will fortify your body, mind and spirit in beneficial ways. Finally, when you use what you have learned actively in your everyday life, you will not lose the lesson but internalize it—literally ingest it.

In the past when doctors visited homes to minister to the sick they carried a well-stocked black doctor's bag with medicines and healing instruments. If you consider this book of epigrams to be part of your medical arsenal for success, you will never be without a handy cure for whatever ails you. Place these vitamins in your success medicine bag. Take a minimum of two "Success Vitamins" daily with plenty of thought. You will be the better for it.

Be Your Very Best Always,
Judy Williamson

Success Vitamins for a Positive Mind

(over 700 Mind Conditioners) by Dr. Napoleon Hill

Help thy brother's boat across and lo!
thine own hath reached the shore.

These proverbs are based on the experience of more than five hundred of the outstanding leaders who have been responsible for the development of the American way of life.

They have been proved sound and practical because they have worked successfully for those who tried them, and they have been reduced to the fewest words possible, for the benefit of all who sincerely wish to find their places in the world.

The collection was prepared especially for students of the philosophy, with the hope that each person who reads it may be enriched in body, mind, and spirit, for, as the great philosopher, Socrates, has said: "*Wisdom adorns riches and softens poverty.*"

Dedicated by

The Author

to

Students Everywhere
who strive to make this world
a better place in which to live.

Author's Preface

This collection of epigrams is a concentrated presentation of the entire Philosophy of Success, prepared for the man who reads as he runs.

Its purpose is to aid men and women in the development of a personal philosophy of life that will bring them economic security and peace of mind in proportion to their desires and talents.

The most important thing in life is harmony in human relationships!

Friction among men is more costly than friction in machinery.

This philosophy, if followed, will condition one's mind to get along with others in a spirit of friendliness. It will give one a success-consciousness which is so essential for material success in every calling.

Life is short, at best! Too short to justify any man in devoting any portion of his time to the creation of friction between himself and others.

One man could not have set the entire world on fire if friction among men had not prepared the way for him. Let us make our association one of harmony and brotherly love; let us get ahead by helping one another in the spirit of the Master as he expressed it in the Sermon On The Mount—"*All things whatsoever ye would that men should do unto ye do you even so unto them.*"

The world has all but emasculated itself through friction among men. For our own sake and the sake of our children let us now reverse the rule of friction and make our portion of the world one of harmony.

The benefits of harmony have been mirrored for us in everything the Creator has given us, save only in the relationships of men.

The stars that hang up there in the heavens move swiftly and silently, but never get out of their paths.

The seasons of the year come and go with harmonious precision, and the sun rises in the East and sets in the West with daily punctuality and harmony.

The beasts of the jungle and the birds of the air go about their duties in a spirit of harmony, serving as a mighty reprimand to men who neglect to respect one another's rights.

The whole world about us cries out in a language we cannot ignore, a language of pain and failure and fear, warning us that God's way is a way of harmony among men! Let us heed this warning before the preset world chaos is followed by greater disaster, for surely no one is so ignorant as not to recognize that the man who injures his neighbor injures himself more, that a day of reckoning must come to every man who tries to GET without first GIVING a fair equivalent in return.

The day of the "go-getter" has passed. The day of the "go-giver" is at hand. This philosophy was taken from the experiences of men who recognized that "He profits most who serves best."

It is a natural and a healthful human instinct for a man to desire to make life pay on the best terms possible. Experience of the most successful men this nation has produced shows clearly that all constructive achievements and all individual success depend upon a positive mental attitude.

And the thing that goes farthest in giving one a positive mental attitude is harmony within one's own mind and harmony in all human relationships.

Harmony calls for self-discipline; a lot of it!

But, the man who takes the time to develop harmony through self-discipline thereby conditions his mind to attract the better things of life which he may set his mind upon.

These proverbs are mind-conditioners!

Read them thoughtfully and make them your own, then observe how other people definitely and quickly give you their friendly cooperation.

It is one of the great mysteries of life that the mind attracts the physical counterpart of that which it dwells upon. Think of others in terms of brotherly love and they will think of you in the same spirit, although they may not always be conscious of the reason why they do so.

The circumstances of a man's life fit the pattern of his mental attitude, just as surely as the sun rises in the East and sets in the West. Make your mental attitude right and lo! the world around you will become harmonious and cooperative. Opportunities for self-advancement will present themselves.

Promotions will come to you voluntarily. Those who dislike you will change their attitude and begin to like you.

Griping may be sometimes justified bit it never pays! For griping is an outward expression of a negative mental attitude. If you can grasp this truth and make use of it you will be as wise as the sages, and rich in values that make life worth living.

You cannot always control other people's actions toward you, but you can and you should control your re-actions toward others, for this will, in time, set the pattern in all your human relationships which will influence others to your way of thinking.

How do I know these truths?

I know them because I have tired them and found that they work!

And, being one who loves his fellowmen, I crave the privilege of sharing these blessings with all who are ready and willing to adopt them and use them.

This book is printed for everyone who will read the epigrams carefully and recognize that they provide sound counsel for those who are willing to give in order to get the values of life that make people successful and happy.

I am a practical realist who has worked his way upward from the bottom by applying the philosophy on which these epigrams are based. I am a humanitarian who sincerely desires to inspire my students with the spirit of harmony and the mental attitude toward one another that will make life a joy and not a burden.

Yours for personal victory,

Dr. Napoleon Hill

*Whatever the mind can
conceive and believe,
the mind can achieve.*

—NAPOLEON HILL

Let us be Thankful for our Blessings

Let us express our gratitude for what we already possess, rather than complain because of what we wish, for it is a well known fact that prayers of gratitude for the blessings one possesses attract still greater blessings.

Let us supplement our present blessings by a spirit of friendly cooperation, remembering that it was this spirit of thought and deed which gave us our American freedom and riches.

Let us encourage leaders to use their talents and their financial resources in making this a greater world, so our children and the yet unborn generations may enjoy blessings and freedom.

Lastly, may it be the prayer of each of us that from among this generation of our youth there shall rise a new corps of leaders who will, by their talents and their personal ambitions, provide us with the sort of opportunities which have been provided in the past by such men as Henry Ford, Thomas A.

Edison, Andrew Carnegie, the Wright Brothers, Capt. Eddie Rickenbacker, Henry J. Kaiser and R. G. LeTourneau.

For these are the sort of men who have given us our way of life—our great system of free enterprise without which we would be no better off than were the primitive children of the wilderness who had this vast undeveloped country before we made it what it is.

Ours is the last outpost of human freedom. Let us keep it so, by our friendly, harmonious cooperation whereby we may walk arm in arm and do our work and reap our just reward in that spirit of humanity so clearly described by the Lord in the Sermon on the Mount.

Remember to express gratitude every day—by prayer and affirmation— for the blessings you have.

—NAPOLEON HILL

Do You Crave Riches?

The richest man in all the world lives over in Happy Valley. He is rich in values that endure; in things that cannot be stolen; things he cannot lose; things that provide him with contentment, sound health, peace of mind and harmony of soul.

This is his description of his riches and how he acquired them:

1. "I found happiness by helping others to find it.
2. "I have sound health because I live temperately in all things and eat only the food that nature requires for body maintenance; foods that are grown from God's Good Earth.
3. "I am free from fear in all its forms.
4. "I hate no man, envy no man, but love all mankind.
5. "I am engaged in a labor of love, with which I mix play generously; therefore, I never grow tired.
6. "I pray daily, not for more wealth, but for more wisdom with which to recognize, embrace and enjoy the great abundance of riches I already possess.

7. "I speak no name save only to honor it, and I slander no man.

8. "I ask no favors of anyone except the privilege of sharing my blessings with all who will receive them.

9. "I am on good terms with my conscience; therefore, it guides me correctly in all that I do.

10. "I have no enemies because I injure no man for any cause, but I benefit all with whom I come into contact, by teaching them the way to all riches.

11. "I have more material wealth than I need because I am free of greed and covet only the material things I can use while I live. My material wealth is provided by those whom I have aided by sharing with them knowledge of my way of life.

12. "The estate of Happy Valley is not taxable because it exists mainly in my own mind, in intangible riches that cannot be assessed except by those who adopt my way of life. I created this vast estate, by observing nature's laws and adopting my habits to harmonize with God's plans, as evidenced by these laws."

These are riches that endure!

They may be shared by all who are willing to emulate the man from Happy Valley.

But emulation requires preparation of the mind, for no one may live in Happy Valley who indulges a negative mind.

The paragraphs that follow may, if you will heed their counsel, prepare you to live in Happy Valley the remainder of your life.

Look in the Mirror

My secretary walked into my office early one morning and announced that a tramp was outside with an urgent request that I see him. At first I decided to save time by sending him the price of a sandwich and a cup of coffee, but something prompted me to have him sent in.

I've never seen a more dilapidated looking man. He had a week's growth of beard and wrinkled clothes that looked as if he had dragged them from a rag pile.

"I don't blame you for looking surprised at my appearance," he began, "but I'm afraid you have me all wrong. I didn't come to see you for a handout. I came to ask you to help me save my life.

"My troubles began a year ago when I had a break with my wife, and we were divorced. Then everything began to go against me. I lost my business, and now I'm losing my health.

"I came to see you at the suggestion of a policeman who stopped me just as I was going to jump in the river. He gave me my choice of coming to see you or going to jail. He's waiting outside to see that I carry out my promise."

The tone of the man's voice and the language he used indicated clearly that he was a man of considerable education. Questioning brought out the fact that he had owned one of the best known restaurants in Chicago. I remembered seeing a news account of it being sold at a sheriff's sale several months previously.

I had my secretary get him a breakfast because he hadn't eaten for two days. While the food was being prepared I got the man's entire life story. Not once did he blame anyone for his condition but himself. That was a sign in his favor and one that gave me my cue as to how I could help him.

After he finished eating I did the talking.

"My friend," I began, "I have listened to your story very carefully and I'm deeply impressed by it. I am especially impressed with the fact that you haven't tried to alibi yourself clear of responsibility for your condition.

"I'm also impressed by the fact that you don't place blame on your former wife for your divorce. You are to be commended for speaking of her in the respectful way that you have."

By this time the man's spirits were rising higher and higher.

The moment had come for me to spring my plan of action and I let him have it in a way that made it register as I had hoped it would.

"You came to me for help" I continued, "but I am sorry to tell you that after hearing your story there is not one thing I can do to help you!"

"But," I continued, "I know a man who can help you if he will do it. He is here in this building right now and I will introduce you to him if you wish me to do so."

Then I took him by the arm and led him into my private study adjacent to my office and told him to stand in front of a long curtain, and as I pulled the curtain aside he saw himself in a full length mirror.

Pointing my finger at the man in the mirror I said, "There is the man who can help you. He is the *only man* who can do it, and until you become better acquainted with him and learn to depend upon him you will not find your way out of your present unfortunate condition."

He walked over closer to the mirror, looked at himself very closely as he rubbed his stubbled face, then turned to me and said, "I see what you mean, and may God bless you for not coddling me."

With that he bowed his way out and I didn't see or hear from him for almost two years when he walked in one day, so changed in appearance that I did not recognize him. He explained that he got the help of the Salvation Army in clothing himself properly. Then he got a job in a restaurant similar to the one he had formerly owned, worked in it as a headwaiter for a time when a former friend met him there by chance, heard his story and loaned him the money with which to buy the place.

He is today one of the more prosperous restaurant owners of Chicago, as rich as he needs to be in money, but richer still in having discovered the power of his own mind and how to use it as a means of contracting and drawing upon the powers of Infinite Intelligence.

In every adversity or defeat there is a seed of an equal or greater benefit.

—NAPOLEON HILL

Render more service and better service than is expected of you if you wish to attract quick and permanent promotion.

−NAPOLEON HILL

Remember that you cannot promote yourself on another man's mistakes and weaknesses, except by helping him to correct them.

No man can become a permanent success without taking others along with him.

It's not what you are going to do, but it's what you are doing now, that counts.

The word "impossible" is not recognized by successful men but it is a handy alibi of the man who is a failure.

———o o———

All rivers and some men are "crooked" because
they take the line of least resistance.

———o o———

A man's efficiency may be accurately judged by
the amount of supervision he requires.

———o o———

Remember that the quality of service you render plus the
quantity, plus the mental attitude in which you render it,
determines the sort of job you hold and the pay you receive.

———o o———

Remember that every defeat and every disappointment and
every adversity carries the seed of an equivalent benefit.

———o o———

The most successful men are those who serve
the greatest number of people.

———o o———

There is something worse than being compelled to work.
It is being compelled not to work.

———o o———

If you wish a job done promptly and well,
get a busy man to do it. The idle man knows
too many substitutes and short cuts.

The man with a negative mental attitude attracts
troubles as an electromagnet attracts steel filings.

Opportunity has a way of getting near the man
with a positive mental attitude.

If you are worried or afraid of anything there is something
in your mental attitude that needs correction.

Cooperation and Friendship are two assets
that can be had only by first giving them.

Remember, a kite flies against the wind, not with it.

Every thought a man releases becomes a
permanent part of his character.

The surest way to promote yourself is
to help others get ahead.

The greatest of all success rules is this:
Do unto others as you would if you were the others.

Remember that no one is ever rewarded or promoted because of a bad disposition and a negative mental attitude.

The man who says "it can't be done" is usually busy trying to keep out of the way of the man who is doing it.

Time is the greatest of all doctors. If given a chance it can cure most of the ills that men gripe about.

No man is capable of giving orders unless he knows how to take orders and carry them out.

When you feel sluggish, try nature's doctor. Just quit eating until you are hungry again.

The man who listens more than he talks generally knows more than the man who talks more than he listens.

Willing cooperation produces enduring power while forced cooperation ends in failure.

Remember that a policeman is the only sort of man who gets satisfactory results with fear and force. Others do better with persuasion.

Fortunate indeed is the man who has learned
to put the spirit of play into his daily work.
He will live longer and earn more.

Anyone can quit when the going is hard,
but a thoroughbred never quits until he wins.

You can't hurt another man's feelings or do
yourself injury by speaking of another's virtues.

No man can get to the top without
carrying others along with him.

Look for the good in others and they
will do the same with you.

If I had but one wish that could be granted, it would be for
more wisdom with which to enjoy the many blessings
I possess under the American form of Government.

This is a fine world for the man who knows precisely
what he wants of life and is busy getting it.

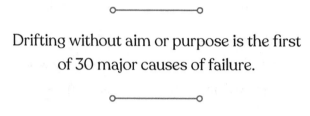

Drifting without aim or purpose is the first
of 30 major causes of failure.

You can't find happiness by robbing another of it.
Ditto as to economic security.

Trying to get without first giving is as fruitless
as trying to reap without having sown.

Luck appears to favor the man who spells the word—p-luck!

What do you want from life and what have you
to give in return that entitles you to it?

Try telling your foreman about the things you like
and see how willingly he will help you get rid of
the things you don't like.

Wise men think twice before speaking once.

Never criticize anything or anyone
unless you are prepared to offer something to
improve that with which you find fault.

Edison failed ten thousand times before he perfected
the modern electric lamp. The average man would
have quit at the first failure. That's why there are
so many "average" men and only one Edison.

There is something good about any man who is
loved by his dog and his family, for they know him as he is.

The successful man keeps his mind fixed on that
which he wants—not that which he doesn't want.

The creator gave each man a conscience for
use as a guide to right conduct. But some have
perverted it into a conspirator instead.

The greatest and the most resultful of all prayers are those
offered as gratitude for the blessings we already have.

It is better to give thanks for the blessings we already
have than to pray for more blessings.

That man is rich indeed who has more friends than enemies,
fears no one, and is so busy building that he has no time to
devote to tearing down another's hopes and plans.

Hatred damages most the one doing the hating.

The end of the rainbow is reached only
at the end of the second mile.

You can't control other men's acts,
but you can control your mental reaction
to their acts and that is what counts most to you.

The man who has only time for gossip and slander is too busy for success.

−NAPOLEON HILL

Some people are so busy failing that they haven't
time to learn the rules of success.

○────────○

That which you think today becomes
that which you are tomorrow.

○────────○

Men like you better when you greet them
with a smile instead of a frown.

○────────○

Chickens come home to roost and so do men's thoughts,
so be careful what sort of thoughts you send out.

○────────○

The orderliness of the world of natural laws gives evidence
that they are under control of a universal plan.

There is harmony throughout the universe, in everything
except human relationships.

Wisdom adorns riches and softens poverty. —SOCRATES.

Friction in machinery costs in terms of money.
Friction in human relations impoverishes
both the spirit and the purse of man.

If you cannot agree with another you can at least
refrain from quarreling with him on that account.

There are three sides to most of your disagreements with
others: your side, the other fellow's side and the right side.
Which may be somewhere between the other two sides.

The man who only does enough work to
"get him by" seldom gets much more than "by."

You can always tell a man who thinks he is smarter
than others, but you can't tell him much.

A temper is a good thing to have provided one does not try
to give it to someone else.

If you must speak ill of another, do not speak it—
write it in the sand near the water's edge.

When everyone else fails you in times of adversity,
try depending on yourself and you may discover
hidden riches of fabulous value in your own mind-power.

Self-praise is a credit only when it consists of deeds
helpful to others and not of mere words.

Isn't it strange that princes and kings
and clowns that caper in sawdust rings
and common folks like you and me
are all builders for eternity.
To each is given a bag of tools,
a block of stone, and a book of rules,
and each must shape, ere time has flown,
a stumbling block or a stepping stone.

If you really are smarter than other men you will
let others find this out from your deeds.

It is always safe to talk about other men
as long as you speak of their good qualities.

No man ever becomes so successful
that he doesn't appreciate a kindly word
of commendation for work well done.

Because he stuck to a single idea, Henry Ford
made himself the head of the world's largest
motor industry and gives profitable employment,
directly and indirectly, to over 10%
of the people of the U.S.A.

If your mind can make you sick—and it can—
remember it also can make you well.

Have you ever thought what a vast difference there is
between what you want and what you actually need for
health and happiness?

Most successful men in the higher brackets
of success did not strike their best stride
until they passed the age of forty.

It will pay anyone to stand on the sideline of life
and watch himself go by now and then,
so he may see himself as the world sees him.

The greatest of all schools is popularly known
as the University of Hard Knocks.

Two kinds of men never get ahead.
Those who do only that which they are told to do
and those who will not do what they are told to do.

The man who doesn't reach decisions promptly
when he has all necessary facts in hand
cannot be depended upon to carry out
decisions after he makes them.

The successful leader makes decisions quickly
but changes them slowly if they must be changed.

The surest winners are those who give you
a "yes" or a "no" without resorting
to that time-worn alibi—"I'll think it over."

Don't be in too big a hurry
to get to the top of the ladder of success,
for then you can move in only one direction—down.

Quick promotions are not always the most enduring.

No man is ever rewarded by promotion
because of a negative mental attitude.

When you have talked yourself into what you want,
right there is the place to stop talking and
begin saying it with deeds.

Your reputation is that which people think you are,
your character is that which you are.

The best job goes to the man who can get it done
without passing the buck or coming back with alibis.

When you waste tools or materials,
you waste also your opportunity
for a better job and more pay.

Unless you are an army officer, you can get better
results by "requests" than you can by "orders."

Look for the good in others and they will look for
the good in you. Ditto as to the "bad."

Most headaches have their source in the sewer system,
as the result of toxic poisoning.

Good credit is a great asset provided it is not over-used.

The moment anyone accepts favors he is in debt to the one
granting them. Sooner or later the debt must be paid.

It is better to imitate a successful man than to envy him.

You either ride life or it rides you. Your mental attitude
determines who is rider and who is "horse."

A truly big man never tries to impress others with his
bigness and never tries to "keep up with the Joneses."

The most interesting thing about a postage stamp is
the persistence with which it sticks to its job.

No man is a free man until he learns
to do his own thinking and gains the courage
to act on his own personal initiative.

The imagination is the workshop of the soul
wherein a man's destiny is fashioned.

Only an open mind can grow.

Dependability is the first foundation stone
of good character.

You can tell by the company a man chooses
what sort of character he has.

Only one thing will attract love and that is love.

—NAPOLEON HILL

Make yourself indispensable at your job and see how quickly you are pushed out of it into a better job.

○───────○

Self-discipline is the first rule of all successful leadership.

○───────○

Watch the man ahead of you and you'll soon learn why he is ahead. Then emulate him.

○───────○

The humblest person of today has conveniences and luxuries kings could not afford a few decades ago.

○───────○

Every scrap-pile and every tool bin
and every operation in this plant
contains a hidden opportunity
for someone to earn more money.
Why not look around?

Work as though the business belonged
to you and some day it may.

Authority that is abused is soon lost.

The "time" you put on a job is not the
correct measure of your worth. That is determined
by the quality and the quantity of your work.
Plus the influence you have on others
by your mental attitude.

If your work is always satisfactory the chances are
a hundred to one your pay will be the same.

If some men where paid only what they are
worth they would starve to death.

Every time you slander another person remember that
someone may say to himself: "sour grapes."

Your employer may not always know
when you have done a poor day's work
but you know, and you are damaged
more than your employer.

Before opportunity crowns a man
with great success it usually tests him
out through adversity to see what
sort of mettle he is made of.

Many men have confused their desires and needs
with their just rights; not always does a man have
a right to many things he needs.

Education means development of
the mind from within, so it will help
one to take his problems apart and
put them to work for him and not
against him. All education is self-acquired
since no one can educate another.

Being the longest on the job does not
necessarily mean that a man earns the biggest wages.

Most automobile accidents are due to discourtesy
and disregard of the other fellow's rights.

Self-respect is the best means
of getting the respect of others.

Suppose you had to help straighten out the trouble
of every person on the works and you'll have a
fair idea of what a manager's job is like.

Every thought you release becomes a
permanent part of your character.

Think in terms of opulence if you wish to attract riches.

Sometimes it is wiser to join forces with
an opponent than it is to fight him.

Sound character is man's greatest asset because
it provides the power with which he may ride the
emergencies of life instead of going down under them.

That which you learn from your job may ultimately be more
valuable to you than the immediate pay you receive.

A peace maker always fares better than an agitator.

If you are not learning while earning you are cheating
yourself of the better portion of your just compensation.

If you become discouraged think of Helen Keller
who, although she is deaf, dumb, and blind,
has made a good living by writing books
to inspire her more fortunate fellowmen.

A blind boy paid his way to a master's degree
in Northwestern University by taking notes
on class lectures, in the Braille system of shorthand,
writing them out on a typewriter and selling
copies to his classmates who had strong eyes
but weak ambition.

Never argue with a pole-cat for he has
a strong argument of his own.

Instead of complaining of that which you don't like
about your job start commending that which you
do like and see how quickly your job will improve.

Birds of a feather flock together.
So do men who try to live by their wits alone.

Just omit your opinions and give me the facts so I may
form my own opinions, and you may serve me better.

Beware of the man who tries to poison your
mind against another under a pretense of
helping you. The chances are a thousand to one
he is trying to help himself.

An opinion is no sounder than the
judgment of the person offering it.

Friendly cooperation will get a man more than
unfriendly agitation, in any market.

Every time you perform any task, try to excel your last
performance and very soon you will excel those around you.

Today's employer is yesterday's employee who found
opportunity waiting for him at the end of the second mile.

Nature yields her most profound secrets to the man
who is determined to uncover them.

Honesty and hard work are commendable
traits of character but they will never make
a success of the man who does not guide them
toward a definite major purpose.

Don't be afraid to aim high when choosing
your life's goal. For no matter how high you aim,
your achievements may fall below it.

There isn't much one can do for the man who
will not try to do something for himself.

The man who does not systematically
save a definite percentage of all he makes is apt
never to acquire economic security.

If one gets something for nothing it generally turns
out to be worth to him about what it cost.

A dog is smart enough to bury a bone for the day
when he will need it. Not so with many men.

It isn't what you earn as much as what you save
that counts in the long run.

Nothing that causes a man to worry
is worth what his worry cost him
in peace of mind and physical health.

The loss caused by friction in human relationships,
if it could be prevented, would make all men
tax free and pay for the world war in a single year.

I glory in your good fortunes and your smartness
provided you don't remind me of them too often.

A man is generally a welcomed visitor at his neighbor's
house as long as he brings glad tidings and refrains
from discussing his troubles.

A man with a yen for using his head was given a check
for $100,000.00 for taking one word out of the name of
a well known breakfast food, which lowered the freight rate
on the product to a saving of double that annually.

The best time to "doctor" is before you become sick.

Two things money cannot buy—
love and friendship. These are
gifts of the Gods and have
no fixed price.

−NAPOLEON HILL

Beware of the man who goes out of his way
to pay you compliments you know you don't
deserve, for he is on the hunt for something
you may not wish to part with.

Flattery is a powerful tool and as old as mankind,
but woe is the lot of the flatterer who uses it
to take unfair advantage of another.

Never accept slanderous talk without first substantiating it
because the slanderer obviously is a biased witness.

A life-long acquaintance is not necessarily a friend.

There are no such realities as good or bad luck.
Everything has a cause that produces appropriate effects.

"Miracle" is a word often misused to describe
a phenomenon that is not understood.

The five known realities of the entire universe
are time, space, matter, energy and the intelligence
that gives these orderliness.

Some men resemble a cheap watch.
They are not dependable.

Do not belittle the practical dreamer
for he is the forerunner of civilization.

Don't take yourself too seriously
if you wish to get any joy out of life.

Defeat may be a stepping stone or a stumbling
block according to the way one accepts it.

When I hear a man running this country down, I wonder
why he doesn't move to one he thinks is better.

When adversity overtakes you
it will pay you to be thankful it was not worse
instead of worrying over your misfortune.

The most interesting subject you can discuss
with most men is—themselves.

Medals and titles will not count when you get to heaven,
but you may be looked over carefully
for the sort of deeds you have done.

No man could ride a horse if the horse discovered
its real strength. Ditto as to a man.

The man who does a good job of getting ready to live
has gone a long way toward getting ready to die.

Count that day lost whose low descending sun
finds you with no good deeds done.

Clothes may not make a man, but they may go
a long way toward giving him a favorable start.

Take possession of your own mind and you may
soon make life pay off on your terms.

Henry Ford's mind is precisely like
every other normal mind, but he used his
to think with and not to harbor
fear and self-imposed limitations.

Remember that the mind grows strong through use.
Struggle makes power.

There is no such reality as passive faith.
Action is the first requirement of all faith.
Words, alone, will not serve.

In a well managed business all promotions are self made.
The employer's only part in the transaction is to check
carefully to make sure the promotion has been earned.

Never mind what you have done in the past.
What are you going to do in the future?

While you are "showing up" others, it may be well
to take a good look at yourself.

Remember, every word you speak
gives someone a chance to find out
how much—or how little—you know.

A man may learn by listening, but not by talking.

Before anything can come out of the mind,
something must be put into it.

If you are looking for trouble, someone will be
meddlesome enough to help you find it.

After you have slandered another,
what have you gained for your pains?

An idle mind is the devil's playground.

Misfortune has a queer habit of showing up
where it is expected.

Isn't it peculiar that a man often is so clever
at inventing alibis and so dull at doing the job
that would make alibis useless?

The law can take away from you everything you possess
except your power of thought.

Haven't you noticed that a man can always find a way
to do that which he must do or else?

If a man worked as hard at the task he desires to do as
he does at the task he must do, he could go places.

Money is either a good or a bad influence, according
to the character of the man who possesses it.

One way to avoid criticism is to do nothing and be
a nobody. The world will then not bother you.

When one man can set the entire world on fire, there must
have been too much dry tinder lying around.

Burn your bridges behind you.
Set your mind on a definite goal and observe
how quickly the world stands aside to let you pass.

If you have a better way of doing anything, your idea may be
worth a substantial fortune.

The man who dipped a chunk of ice cream in chocolate
and called it "Eskimo Pie" made a fortune for the
five seconds of imagination required to create the idea.

Henry Ford is reported to have offered twenty-five
thousand dollars to anyone who would show him how to
save a single bolt and nut on each automobile he makes.

Find out how to get production up and it will drag you
and a bigger pay check along with it.

Who told you it couldn't be done, and what great
achievement has he performed that qualified him to
set up limitations for you?

How can you judge others accurately if you have
not learned to judge yourself accurately?

If you don't know, have the courage to admit it and
you will be well on the road toward learning.

When angry, whistle for three minutes before speaking and
observe how your anger will take on the quality of reason.

Go to bed praying and get up singing and
notice what a fine day's work you will do.

There can never be any harm in speaking about other
people provided you speak of their good qualities.

Remember the tone of your voice often conveys more
accurately what is in your mind than do your words.

Have you ever tried to be angry while you were smiling? Try it!

—NAPOLEON HILL

When a man says: "They say" so and so.
Ask him to name who "they" are
and watch him squirm with embarrassment.

o———o

Columbus didn't know where he was going
when he started, didn't know where he was
when he got there, nor where he had been
when he returned. So his neighbors had him
chained in prison on suspicion.

o———o

You cannot make all people like you,
but you can rob them of a sound reason
for disliking you.

o———o

"How do you know" is a question that has put many
talkative persons out on a limb for an answer.

Look carefully if the pasture on the other side
of the fence appears greener, for there may be
plenty of thistles mixed with the grass.

Today's dreams become tomorrow's realities.

A man without a definite major purpose is as
helpless as a ship without a compass.

Profanity is a sign of inadequate vocabulary
or unsound judgment, or both.

Boastfulness generally is an admission
of an inferiority complex.

Everything one needs or desires has a way
of showing up as soon as one is ready for it.
"Ready" doesn't mean "wish."

Light travels at a speed of 186,000 miles per second,
but thought can travel much faster. It can go
from the mind to the sun, 93,000,000 miles
in a fraction of a second, and nothing can stop it.

The keenest minds are those which have been
whetted most by practical experience.

"Faith can move mountains." So can perspiration
if it is aided by a LeTourneau Scraper.

Temperament is a state of mind consisting of nine
parts "temper" and one part "mental" energy.

Many men have found opportunities
in failure and adversity which they
could not recognize in the more
favorable circumstances.

Some men appear to be "allergic" to honest work,
but opportunity is equally allergic to them.

"Smart guys" have two words for it.
The words are "so what?"

Ponder the fact that one has
complete control over but one thing,
and that is the power of one's own thoughts.

A man may get to the top by "pull,"
but he can stay there only by "push."

Never fear unjust criticism, but be sure it is unjust.

Many men have found opportunities in
failure and adversity which they could not recognize
in the more favorable circumstances.

Time is a wonderful healer. It tends to equalize
good and evil and to right the wrongs of the world.

Happiness is found in doing—not merely in possessing.

Tell me how you use your "spare" time and I will tell
you what and where you will be ten years hence.

You will never need to discipline yourself as closely while
you are on the way up as you will when you get on top.

The depression taught us that there is something
infinitely worse than being forced to work.
It is being forced not to work.

Anyone can stand poverty,
but few can stand success and riches.

Remember that every time you go the extra mile you
place someone under obligation to you.

Pick out some person whom you admire
and imitate him or her as closely as you can.
This is hero-worship, but it improves character.

If you must be deceitful, be sure you never try to
deceive your best friend—yourself.

You will find time for all your needs if you
have your time properly organized.

A fool may stumble upon opportunity,
but the wise man goes out looking for it.

You might discover how to save enough
time and materials in your department to
insure you an increase in pay and a better job.
Why don't you try?

Some men succeed if they are encouraged.
Others succeed in spite of hell and high water.
Take your choice.

It is better to let a man earn something
he deserves than to give it to him.

Making life "easy" for children
usually makes life "hard" for them in adulthood.

A dull headache usually means
a sluggish sewer system—your sewer system.

Eat right, think right, sleep right,
and play right and you can
save the doctor's bill
for your vacation money.

When things become so bad they cannot
become worse they usually begin to be better.

You can fatten hogs on sawdust—if you mix enough
corn with it. The more corn the better.

Ferdinand the Bull has some good qualities
but you can't bring them out by shaking
a red cloth in his face. Ditto as to men.

Remember that most troubles men get into
overtake them when they are in bad company
or at places where they should not be.

Don't overlook small details. Remember that
the universe and all that is in it is made from atoms,
the smallest known particles of matter.

Did you cheat the other fellow, or yourself?
Be thoughtful before you answer.

Your ship will not come in unless you have first sent it out.

Remember that most troubles men get into
overtake them when they are in bad company
or at places where they should not be.

No man is so good that he has no bad in him,
and no man is so bad that he has no good in him.

Meddlesome curiosity is one of the major causes of failure.

You could be wrong now and then, you know.

A highly cultured person grants favors
graciously or not at all.

Able leaders have no use for "yes" men.

Fat people may be good natured,
but they sometimes die too young.

Most failures could have been converted
into successes if someone had held on
another minute or made one more effort.

Never criticize anything you don't understand.
Better put in the time trying to learn something about it,
then criticism may be unnecessary.

> The amount of supervision a
> man requires is a fair measure
> of the value of his services.
>
> —NAPOLEON HILL

You fit perfectly somewhere in life.
Keep on searching until you find where.

○———○

If you don't know what you want from life,
what do you think you will get?

○———○

That man is truly wise who knows
how very little he knows, all told.

○———○

What can you do that a dozen others
whom you know cannot do as well or better?

○———○

If inventors feared criticism we would still be
traveling by ox cart and wearing homespun clothing.

Unlimited power may be available when two
or more men coordinate their minds and
deeds in a spirit of perfect harmony
for the attainment of a definite purpose.

It is more beneficial to ask intelligent questions than it is
to offer free opinions which have not been requested.

If this is not the finest and best country on earth,
why are you living here?

When you ask another person to do something,
it may help both him and you if you tell him:
What to do
Why he should do it
When he should do it
Where he should do it
and
How he may best do it.

Be sure about what you want from life and doubly sure
as to what you have to give in return.

An educated man is one who has learned how to get what
he wants without violating the rights of others.

If you want accurate answers to questions,
do not disclose the sort of answer you expect
since most people try to please.

You never know who are your real friends until adversity
overtakes you and you need financial cooperation.

Success attracts success and failure attracts failure
because of the Law of Harmonious Attraction.

It is better to go down to defeat fighting
than never to have put up a fight, for that
proves you have the right stuff for a comeback.

Too much self-confidence often inspires too little caution.

Don't quit when the going is hard.
If you must quit, wait until you can quit a winner.

The best way to get favors is to start handing out favors.

Just imagine what it would feel like if your automobile radio,
refrigerator and electric lights were taken away from you.

The best way to fight the imaginary person
called the "Devil" is by serving his opponent.

Some men are "smart," others are "wise."
The difference is this: the "smart" man can make money,
the "wise" man can make it and use it wisely.

Which would you prefer to give up—
all your friends or all your money?

It is not true that "all men are born equal."
But it is true that they are born with equal rights.

Happiness may be had only by helping others to find it.

A man in prison may have privileges, but he has no rights.
These were forfeited to the law by his misfortune.

No man can succeed and remain successful
without the friendly cooperation of others.

The things a man actually needs are few. They are one suit
of clothes, one bed and enough food to sustain his body.

There would be an over abundance of everything
men need or could use intelligently if some
did not try to get more than they need.

Don't be too hard on your subordinate,
for he may become your superior later on.

Procrastination is the bad habit of putting off
until day after tomorrow that which
should have been done day before yesterday.

The habitual procrastinator always is
an expert creator of alibis.

The man who is quick to see his limitations
generally is slow in seeing his opportunities.

If you were your own employer, would you be entirely
satisfied with the day's work you have done today?
Honor bright?

Men don't mind being told of their faults if one is generous
enough to mix in a few of their virtues as well.

You are where you are and what you are because
of the food you eat and the thoughts you think.

If you were offered the best job on the works
are you ready to fill it?

Opportunity has a queer way of stalking the person
who can recognize it and is ready to embrace it.

The most profitable time any man spends
is that for which he is not directly paid.

Your best friend may be the fellow who tells you
bluntly what is wrong with you.

The man who wastes his own time may be no less a thief
than the man who steals other people's property.

The man who is honest for a "price"
only should be rated as dishonest.

A man without enthusiasm
is like a watch without a mainspring.

The truly great man is a servant—not a master.

A lazy man is either sick or one who has not found
the work he likes best.

Your mental attitude determines
the sort of friends you attract.

The man who has more enemies than friends
needs to examine his own mental attitude.

The world stands aside and makes room for the person
who knows where he is going and is on his way.

Be still a few minutes each day and let the great soul
within you speak to you from within.

The most important job is that of learning how
to negotiate with others without friction.

Three little words—"if you please"—
carry the power of great charm.

Not always is it what you say,
as much as the way you say it, that counts.

Have you noticed how natural it is for a man to modify
his tone of voice so it pleases when he asks for a favor?

The greatest known cure for loneliness,
discouragement and discontentment
is work that produces a healthy sweat.

The greatest among men are those who serve the greatest number.

—NAPOLEON HILL

The man who tries to promote himself by demoting others cannot stay on top if he gets there.

Remember, it is not necessary for others to fail in order that you may succeed.

Keep your mind open and remember that no one knows the last word about anything.

Self-confidence may be mistaken for egotism if it is not accompanied by humility of the heart.

With all your getting, be sure to get a good stock of common courtesy.

A man who is at peace with himself
is also at peace with the world.

You can do it if you believe you can!

Become acquainted with your other self!
It may be better than the one you know best.

Prayer expressed with fear or doubt
always produces only negative results.

One great lesson to be learned from a dog
is that of enduring loyalty.

Loyalty to those to whom loyalty is due is the first
foundation stone of sound character.

No man can be trusted who has not within him
the quality of inherent loyalty.

High wages and the capacity to assume
responsibilities are two things that belong together.

Success requires no explanations—
failure must be doctored with alibis.

There is a vast difference between failure and
temporary defeat. No one may succeed
until he recognizes the nature of this difference.

Even a chicken enjoys scratching for food
in the straw, which it believes to be hidden.
Remember that men, too, like to discover
your virtues in their own way.

A man is never a failure until he accepts
defeat as permanent and quits trying.

The only real limitation of the human mind
is that which a man sets up in his own mind.

Victory is always possible for the person
who refuses to stop fighting.

Remember, it takes at least two people
to carry on a quarrel.

Deeds, not words, are the greatest means of self praise.

Lead pencils have erasers because
all men sometimes make mistakes.

Men with a clear conscience seldom fear anything.

The only permanent thing in the entire universe is change.
Nothing is the same for two consecutive days.

Never express an opinion unless you can
explain how you came by it.

The man who does no more
han he is paid for has no real basis
for requesting more pay because
he is already getting all he is earning.

Most opinions are mere hopeful wishing,
and not the result of careful analysis of facts.

The safest and best way to punish one
who has done you an injustice
is to do him a kind deed in return.

If you don't have the full approval of your
conscience and your reason, you had better not
do the thing you contemplate.

Before trying to master others,
be sure you are the master of yourself.

If a man gave spoken expression to every thought that
comes into his mind, he would have no friends.

If you are really great you will let others
discover this fact from your deeds.

Falsehood doth evermore have a way of publishing itself.

If you would have good health,
learn to quit eating before you are entirely satisfied.

A man is either honest or dishonest.
There can be no compromise between the two.

A man comes finally to believe anything
he tells himself often enough, even if it be not true.

Mutual confidence is the major foundation
of all satisfactory human relationships.

The man who tries to get something for nothing
generally winds up getting nothing for something.

The man who gambles for money is a potential cheater,
for he is trying to get something for nothing.

A "successful" politician is one who is long on promises,
but short on keeping them.

Don't be afraid of criticism, but be prepared to
accept it if you have a brand new idea to offer.

The scientist is the only type of man who does no hopeful
wishing and accepts all the facts as he finds them.

Never engage in any transaction which does not benefit,
as nearly equally as possible, all whom it affects.

No man is properly educated until he has read
Emerson's essays and understands them.

A "sharp" bargain often turns out to be
a boomerang for the man who makes it.

A good teacher is always a good student.

It is more beneficial to do more
than you are paid for than to do less.

Never ask a favor of anyone unless you have first
earned the right to expect it will be granted.

The second mile—the one for which you are not paid—
generally yields more returns in the long run
than the first mile.

Never criticize another man's deeds unless you know
why he expressed them. The chances are you would
have done the same under the same circumstances.

Every bargain based on fear or force is
a bad bargain for the one who drives it.

Some nuggets of thought are worth
more than nuggets of gold.

The art of being grateful for the blessings you already
possess is of itself the most profound form of worship,
and incomparable gem of prayer.

Remember, the man whom you believe to be laughing
at your profane jokes may be laughing at you instead.

If you can't take criticism, you have no right
to dish it out to others.

> # It is better to request a man to perform a service than it is to order him to perform it.
>
> —NAPOLEON HILL

The two most important things to every man in this plant are time and materials, for they contain the fundamentals of opportunity for every man who uses them wisely.

○———————○

"Soldiering" on company time may
fool the management for a while, but is open
affrontery to the self respect of all who do it.

○———————○

A wise man asks questions more freely
than he tries to answer them.

○———————○

If you must explode your emotions,
try to pick a time and place
where no one else will be hurt.

The supervisor who doesn't supervise himself
more strictly than he supervises others will not long
remain a supervisor. (Make a mental note of this one
and remind yourself of it before the hammer falls).

Failure is not a disgrace if you have sincerely done your best.

The supervisor who isn't on the job all the time is a poor
example to those who look to him for guidance.

The man who deliberately gets in the way
of opportunity by being on the job all the time
sooner or later is crowned by opportunity.

A good fisherman goes out of his way
to bait his hook with that which fish prefer,
which might not be a bad tip for those
who wish to succeed in human relationships.

Cooperation must start at the head of a department if it is
expected at the other end. Ditto as to Efficiency.

The man who doesn't hand out more favors than he receives
from others will soon find himself "favor bankrupt."

The greatest of all gifts is the gift of an opportunity
for one to help himself.

The one and only thing any man has to give in return
for the material riches he desires is useful service.

Henry Ford became rich, not from the sale of Ford cars,
but the service he rendered through his cars.

Opportunity has a yen for hanging around
in the way of the person who is doing his best.

The man who works in a 100% war production plant
is no less a soldier than the man on the fighting front,
and no less essential.

Think! One hundred and fifty men turn out ten scrapers
per day that do the work of 10,000 men per day.
One scraper less per day kills the work of 1000 men.
–"Uncle Sam"

Pull may help a man to the top but it can't keep him there.
Do the essential job first if you must put off
something until "tomorrow."

Time ultimately cures all the ills and rights the wrongs
of the world. Nothing is impossible with time.

An educated person is not necessarily
the one who has the knowledge, but the one
who knows where to get it when he needs it.

Suspense is the child of indecision,
and it is the first cousin of procrastination.
It is also the "pet" that keeps many people in poverty.

It will do no good to "stop, look and listen"
unless you also think.

Edison failed 10,000 times before
perfecting the incandescent electric light bulb.
Don't worry if you fail once.

Every time you influence another person to do a better job
you benefit him and increase your own value.

If you do a job another man's way he takes the responsibility.
If you do it your way, you must take the responsibility.

If you wish "acquaintanceship," be rich.
If you wish friends, be a friend.

Learn to do one thing better than anyone else
can do it and you can forget your financial problems.

The mistakes others make may provide you with
opportunity for advancement, provided you are
a close observer of little things.

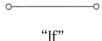

"If"

1. If you can create a plan to save the breakage of tools,
2. If you can find out how to make a pair of gloves last longer,
3. If you can create a short cut that will save time on any operation in the plant,
4. If you can show an associate worker how to save time,
5. If you can make any dangerous jobs safer,
6. If you can help your foreman get more production,
7. If you create a saving of any materials used in the plant,

You can promote yourself
to a better job and more pay.

The job you like least to do
may provide you with the experience
you need for promotion to a better job.

Today's worries may become
tomorrow's priceless experiences.

Be dependable, be willing to assume responsibilities,
be on hand always, be loyal, be courteous,
be willing to help others get ahead
and you will be practically sure to
become financially independent.

The best possible way to get a transfer
from the job you don't like to one you like better
is to do your present job so well the management
will desire to use your skill on a more important job.

If you are not trying to learn all about
your foreman's job, you are tossing away the
possibility of promotion to his or a better job.

If you wish sound health give your mind orders
to build and maintain a health-consciousness.

Begin looking for symptoms of illness and
disease itself will soon put in its appearance.

A poverty-consciousness cannot bring you riches.

A quick decision usually denotes an alert mind.

Make your money work for you
and you'll not have to work so hard for it.

It's mighty easy for one to justify dishonesty
if he makes his living from it.

It is well to be wise
provided one allows others to discover
his wisdom in their own way.

Man seldom begins to succeed in the higher brackets
of success until he is past forty, mainly because most of his
early years are spent in un-learning things that aren't true.

Definiteness of opinion without tolerance
generally turns out to be only stubbornness.

Another man's mistakes may be a rich field of opportunity
for you if you know what caused his mistakes.

There has always been a shortage of men who get
the job done on time without excuses or grumbling.

No matter what you are or what you do, the world
will find you out as long as you have neighbors.

If you haven't the willpower to keep your physical body
in repair you lack, also, the power of will to maintain
a positive mental attitude in other important
circumstances that control your life.

It is more profitable to be a go-giver than a go-getter.

—NAPOLEON HILL

Men will lend both money and favors to those whom they are sure will repay.

○———○

Studying another man for constructive ideas pays off better than looking for his faults.

○———○

Bankers often lend money on character, but seldom on reputation alone for they have learned that not all reputations are deserved.

○———○

Success attracts success as evidenced by the fact that you can get what you want when you don't need it, more easily than when you are in urgent need.

○———○

The man who jumps at conclusions before he examines the facts usually lands on the wrong end.

When a stranger appears too eager to do something
for you, take care that he doesn't do something to you.

Only those who have the habit of going the second mile
ever find the end of the rainbow.

A sick mind is more dangerous than a sick body,
for it is a form of sickness which is always contagious.

Waste no words on a man who dislikes you.
Deeds will impress him more.

Do your job precisely as if you were your own boss,
and sooner or later you will be!

Big pay and little responsibility are
circumstances seldom found together.

Knowledge is not power. It is only potential power
that becomes real through use.

By all means tell the world how good you are,–
but, first show it!

One bad habit often spoils a dozen good ones.

Speaking out of turn may ease your pride but it may
also play hell with your opportunities.

Satan's soldiers are often found masquerading
in the uniform of his opposition.

When you don't know what else to do with your problem,
try sleeping on it for a night or so.

Courage often is only one jump ahead of fear.

A friendly conscience is a mighty good cure
for sleeplessness.

"Professional joiners" are useful in terms of dues.

The highway to failure is liberally plastered with detour
sign-boards reading—"if—but—impossible—maybe."

If you don't believe it yourself don't ask anyone else to do so.

Steer away from the person
who sees only the faults of others
for he has a few of his own that may be contagious.

Both heaven and hell consist here and now
in the deeds of men.

The time some men devote to giving others a bad
reputation might be better spent in doctoring their own.

People seldom trust the person who doesn't trust himself.

Don't push the other fellow around
if you have corns on your toes.

The man with sound character
generally does not worrying over his reputation.

People who glory in soiling another's reputation generally
have none of their own that is not tarnished.

Attend well to your character
and your reputation will look out for itself.

Defeat will respect you more
if you learn to accept it without fear!

It isn't defeat, but it's your mental attitude
toward it that whips you.

The length of time a man sticks to a job
is a pretty accurate measure of his dependability.

Neither a dog nor a mule has any respect
for the person who fears it.

Epigrams are vitamin pills for mental anemics.

You may learn many useful facts
by studying the honey bee provided
you don't try to show it how to do its job.

The successful man somehow manages to be "out" when
worry comes around and "in" when opportunity visits.

Imagine yourself having to neighbor with a man who had
everything he wanted and had never known defeat.

An over-loaded stomach has
no means of defense except a stomach ache.

The other fellow's mistakes are a weak alibi for your own.

If you can't stand criticism you may as well not
begin anything that is new.

The man who creates good fellowship among men
will never be short of friends.

It is not difficult to forgive the mistakes of the
man who repentfully admits them.

The person who freely confesses his mistakes to his own
conscience will always be on good terms with it.

All necessary means to an end
are justifiable if the end itself is just.

A man without self discipline is as dangerous
as an automobile running down hill
without brakes or steering wheel.

Before force fails try kindly persuasion.

Control your own mind and you may never
be controlled by the mind of another.

To make careless mistakes is bad;
to conceal them by falsehoods is worse.

The man who trusts no other person
doesn't trust himself.

Act on your own initiative, but be prepared
to assume full responsibility for your acts.

Remember that nothing has any value
except that fixed in the mind.

When everything goes dead wrong,
remember there is still a tomorrow.

Kindness applied in a practical way has cured
more crime than has punishment.

Any transaction based on fear or coercion
is unprofitable for all who are affected by it.

Any transaction based on fear or coercion
is unprofitable for all who are affected by it.

It is best not to accept any favor
that is not granted willingly.

You can always see in other people
whatever traits of character you are looking for.

When you get yourself
under complete control,
you can be your own boss.

–NAPOLEON HILL

Maybe it's your dark glasses
and not the world that looks black.

o———o

Confidence is the invisible cement
that makes human relationships stick.

o———o

One food of which one cannot over-eat is fresh fruit.

o———o

What did your conscience have to say
when you punched "out" your time card today?

o———o

Constantly tell a child how "bad" it is and it will just
as constantly strive to live up to its reputation.

Child discipline should begin with parental discipline.

If you don't want a bad reputation,
don't be caught with bad company.

The man who advertises his own virtues
thereby indicates his fear as to their quality.

Some men find it easier and more profitable to work
their fellow workers than to work themselves.

The man who has learned how to live without working
takes great care not to disclose his secret to others.

Never stab a man in the back
nor kick a mule on the wrong end
unless you are prepared for a hard jolt.

Remember that a dog that brings a bone will also
carry back a bone. Ditto as to men who carry tales.

Don't be too ready to judge any man
by the estimation of his enemies.

The ladder of success is never crowded at the top.

There is no meaner man than he whose profession
is that of disturbing, for a price, the harmonious
relationships among others.

Persistence is the outgrowth of self-discipline.

If you don't discipline yourself,
you are sure to be disciplined by others.

The man who hasn't tested his belief
by the rules of logical common sense
may as well be prepared to change it.

When a free-thinker is born,
the devil trembles with fear.

Don't fool yourself! Minorities rule the world,
and how fortunate for the world.

Some people who can't be good
have cunning capacity for being careful.

If you are as smart as a crow,
you know more than some men.

Spoken words leave impressions,
printed words leave tracks.

Prayer through a loud speaker is heard
no sooner than a prayer in silent thought.

Eloquence of words never embellishes prayer,
but sincerity of purpose and faith do.

Don't mistake friendship
for a license to take undue liberties.

Acquaintanceship may develop rapidly,
but friendship is made of time-seasoned stuff.

Beware of too many gifts
lest they turn out to be too costly.

The man who can give his employer a good reputation
nearly always is given a good reputation by his employer.

Wouldn't this be one hell-of-a-world if every one
of us said and did everything he wanted to?

It isn't always the man who starts trouble
who finishes the job.

Riches improperly used become liabilities!

The man who lives right the first half of his life
has a chance to enjoy the last half,
and vice versa.

A spider spinning its web has more
definiteness of purpose than do most men.

Many men who are on their good behavior at home
become their real selves in a strange crowd.

Be sure that your book of life isn't recorded in red ink.

It's better to break an employer's tools
than to break his confidence by hiding the pieces.

Epigrams aren't intended as teachers,
but to inspire thought.

When a strange dog comes up and licks your hand,
Brother you've been complimented.

Do whatever you're going to do
and talk about it afterward.

Never condemn a spoiled child,
for children don't spoil without adult aid.

Be always up and doing but,
be careful what you are doing.

Too much truth will make some men
madder than too little.

Unintentional mistakes may be forgiven
if they don't happen too often.

It's usually some fool who can't swim
that rocks the boat.

Love is just a game to an old bachelor,
but it's a tonic to an old maid.

Your opinion may be safer
if you don't express it as fact.

It's always a young fox that puts
its nose in the skunk's business.
The old fellows know better from experience.

When a dog howls he is sad,
when he wags his tail he is glad,
when he growls he is mad. Quite a vocabulary!

A bee has a pointed argument
against interference with its business.

The man who thinks he can buy his way
into heaven with money alone may regret
that he didn't convert it into good deeds instead.

The more you discipline yourself
the less you will be disciplined by others.

Never start arguing unless
the point you hope to gain
is worth the cost of an argument.

Don't argue with a fool
for he will not know when you win.

The person who loves harmony
usually knows how to maintain it.

Constancy of purpose is the first principle of success.

Living without a definite major purpose
promises nothing but a scant living.

Opportunity will let you down if you aren't strong enough to hold it up.

—NAPOLEON HILL

Trying to convince a man who
doesn't think is love's labor lost.

If you don't feel a thrill of joy
when you see the boss coming your way
there's something wrong with
one or the other or both of you.

No job is big enough to hold up a man
who can't hold up the job.

If you must gripe in order to be happy,
in heaven's name do it in a whisper
so you'll not disturb others.

A man's best recommendation is that which he gives himself
by rendering superior service, in the right mental attitude.

Clarence Saunders made four million dollars in four years
by borrowing the self-help cafeteria idea for the grocery
business and naming it Piggly-Wiggly. Imagination pays!

The Law of Compensation isn't always swift,
but it is as sure of operation as the setting of the sun.

So live today that you can look tomorrow
in the eye without flinching.

Respect the rights of others more
and you'll need to protect your own less.

The person who thinks before he acts
seldom has to apologize for his acts.

If you fight for something, be sure it is worth fighting for.

Let the other fellow win the argument
provided you get what you want by keeping quiet.

The best time to get your side across
is after the other fellow has talked himself out.

Every gift you receive carries with it
a responsibility equivalent to its value.

Wise men often allow their opposition to talk itself to death.

Life never is sweet to the man who is sour on the world.

Say it with deeds and words will be unnecessary.

True wisdom begins with
self-understanding based on self-discipline.

Honesty is a spiritual quality
that cannot be evaluated in terms of money.

The person who gives no mercy may not expect
to receive mercy when he needs it most.

Might throws itself on the side of those who believe in right.

○———————○

The imagination is the workshop of the soul wherein
is shaped all plans for individual achievement.

○———————○

Sometimes the man whom you think you have bested
by talk has outwitted you by silence.

○———————○

If you expect something for nothing
you are doomed for disappointment.

○———————○

Never argue over unimportant details
for if you win you will have gained no advantage.

○———————○

Great achievement is born of struggle.

○———————○

You'll not get much out of life
if you allow others to live it for you.

○———————○

Success that comes easily is apt to go quickly.

○———————○

Growth through struggle is nature's inescapable plan.

○———————○

If your hopes for tomorrow aren't brighter than
your regrets of yesterday you aren't living right!

If you prefer to be a follower pick a winner as your leader,
then keep up with him.

Labor without imagination has a fixed
market price for each class of work.
When mixed with imagination the
price of labor may be without a limit.

Show me one person—just one—
who has succeeded permanently
without putting more into his work
than he took out of it in pay.

Experience has proved that men who think
their way through life fare better than those
who try to force their way through.

Willpower is the outgrowth of definiteness
of purpose expressed through persistent
action based on personal initiative.

Nothing great was ever achieved
without a positive mental attitude.

Singleness of purpose is the secret of all
successful achievements.

Remember, the poorest sort of workman
can do enough to "get him by" but that is all he can get.

Get on good terms with yourself
and see how quickly others get on good terms with you.

The man who starts at the top
is greatly handicapped because then
he can move in but one direction–downward.

Never stop to think about your worries
for they will catch up with you
quickly enough unless you outrun them.

Don't be satisfied with being good at your job.
Be the best and you'll soon be indispensable.

If your word isn't good your bank account may be bad.

Knowledge, intelligently used, attracts greater knowledge.

A smiling face often defeats the cruelest of antagonists, for it is hard to argue with the man who smiles when he speaks.

The greatest of all abilities
is the power to inspire confidence among men.

Isn't it peculiar that people who complain most
find life the hardest?

The greatest judges and ablest thinkers always follow the habit of tempering justice generously with mercy.

Forgiveness, with mental reservations,
is no forgiveness at all.

Some men who believe themselves
to be wise are merely smart.

The records of the universe are so accurately kept that no man can cheat or be permanently cheated except by himself.

The sternest master is the one who never learned to obey.

The harshest judge is the man who is
a stranger to his own conscience.

Hatred spreads like wild weeds in a garden,
without cultivation. Love must be nursed
and cultivated or it will perish of starvation.

Give another person
an opportunity to benefit
himself and you thereby
increase your own.

–NAPOLEON HILL

The more successful man's
philosophy of economy is applied
by increasing his earning capacity
rather than cutting his expenses
to the "poverty-complex" point.

Happiness can be multiplied by
sharing it with others without diminishing
the original source. It is the one asset
which increases when it is given away.

Close the door of fear behind you
and see how quickly the door to faith
will open in front of you.

The ten great success rules are:

1. Keep your mind positive
2. Know what you want
3. Plan your work and work your plan
4. Go the second mile in all human relationships
5. Move on your personal initiative
6. Observe small details but don't let them floor you
7. Be persistent and firm but courteous
8. Regard your work as a part of your religion
9. Be grateful for all your blessings
10. Apply the Golden Rule in all relationships with others

No man is free who holds a grudge against another,
for he is under bond to his own emotions.

Don't be too hard on the "Boss"
for you may be a "Boss" yourself some day.

Poverty may not be a disgrace,
but surely it is not a recommendation.

The man who unjustly injures another is always hurt
worse than the injured, for he thereby thrusts himself
under the relentless weight of his own conscience.

When the going is hardest, just keep on keeping on and you'll get there sooner than some who find the going easy.

Many a parent has made life hard for his children by trying, too zealously, to make it easy for them.

If you cannot sleep have a look at your stomach or a confidential talk with your conscience.

Don't look to the stars for the course of your misfortunes. Look to yourself and get better results.

Curiosity is a great help provided it doesn't poke around where it has no right to go.

Don't try to be a comedian unless you are being paid for your efforts.

It's safer to pull one's own hair when angry than to step on another's toes.

All enduring success is founded upon harmonious human relationships.

Speak gently and you will not need
to weigh your words so carefully.

When estimating the power of an enemy
don't overlook his friends.

Most animals have one virtue that men do not possess.
They never kill or steal except in self-defense
or for the protection of their young.

Don't buy a bond with the money you save by using
"Whoosit's" toothpaste. Buy two bonds with the money you
save by using a pinch of table salt instead.

A wise man watches his faults more closely than his virtues.
Others reverse the order.

If you borrow money, go to your fiends only as a last resort,
if you value friendship above money.

The doctor habit is a regular disease with some people.

Time will cure many ailments which doctors cannot.

Never jump at a conclusion until you are sure
it has a sound foundation.

Thinking your way through your problems
is safer than wishing your way through.

Some men have learned to use the winds of adversity
to sail their ship of life.

Unless you have peace of mind, you are not a free person.

Unfed worry soon dies of starvation.

If you think you are sick you are.

The man who tells a lie will fool himself
by believing it if he tells it often enough.

Hurting another man's reputation will add nothing to your
own, so why bother yourself without compensation.

The man who calls on his friends only when he goes
after something soon finds himself without friends.

Carelessly expressed words
often have an embarrassing rebound.

A man is born with some inalienable right,
but his privileges he must earn.

High taxes with plenty of freedom
are more desirable than no taxes without freedom.

Poets may rave about "love in a cottage"
but others know that love goes out the back door
when poverty knocks at the front door.

If your conscience isn't clear
you'd better start house-cleaning from within.

A free man fears nothing.

The misfortune you wish for others
may become the pattern of your own life.

If you must let someone down be sure it isn't the person
who has trusted you, for a broken trust is hard to repair.

Sound character begins with keen self-respect.

Fear is the devils greatest weapon
and man's greatest enemy.

Freedom and fear cannot co-exist in any person's life.

The best of anything is the cheapest in the long-run.

If you must meddle in human relationships
try to be a peace-maker among men
and you'll not find too much competition.

If you become nervous when the boss comes around
there is something wrong that needs correction.

If you are doing a good job you'll feel happy
when the boss looks you over.

Sooner or later the world will find you out
and reward you or penalize you
for exactly what you are.

o——————o

Justice has the uncanny habit of catching up with people
when they are the least prepared for it.

o——————o

Justice often exacts payment
in the values one dislikes most to part with.

o——————o

What justice lacks in speed is often off-set
by what it doesn't lack in firmness
of decision and certainty of arrival.

o——————o

Justice keeps an accurate record of all debits and credits
and it balances its books with regularity if not with speed.

o——————o

> ## Patience, persistence and perspiration make an unbeatable combination for success.
>
> —NAPOLEON HILL

Anything that disturbs harmony among men is apt
to have originated with those who profit by mistrust.

———o———o———

Friendly cooperation is never any part of the devil's work.
He is working the other side.

———o———o———

Wish no misery on any one lest your wish bounce back
and hit you where it will hurt most.

———o———o———

When you bargain with another person to get
something for nothing, don't forget that the devil
is in on the deal, holding all the winning cards.

———o———o———

The more you are promised for nothing
the less you will get for something.

Never bear down too hard on a man
just because he is subject to your authority,
for the order of the authority sometimes is reversed.

When you get another man told,
be sure you don't tell him too much
for your own good.

The fellow who thinks the whole world is wrong
might be surprised at what the world thinks of him.

When the impulse to take something for nothing strikes
you, think of Adolph Schicklegruber before you act.

It's time enough to "order" a man
after he has refused to act upon a polite request.

It is better to expect too much of yourself than too little.

Character is accurately reflected in one's mental attitude.

Searching for symptoms often leads
to physical and mental illness.

Some men "gripe" when they have a just cause
and others just gripe.

This isn't your country if you are unwilling
to make sacrifices to protect it.

Don't blame children who are bad.
Blame those who failed to discipline them.

Live right on Sunday and you'll feel like showing up
on your job on Monday.

When you don't know anything good to say about a man
just button up your lip and you'll feel better.

When an impulse to knock someone hits you,
knock the impulse instead.

Examine most carefully the things you desire most.

The man who works harder when the boss isn't around
is headed straight for a better job.

When you start giving out you'll soon begin taking in.

If you are bigger than your job,
why don't you lift your job up to your size?

Many men who think they have arrived are surprised to
learn that they have been traveling in the reverse gear.

A truly good workman always is good to his tools
and machinery.

The chances are ten to one that you are potentially
as capable as Henry Ford was at your age excepting
only the difference in your mental attitude and his.

Work must have been provided as a blessing since
every living creature must work or perish.

Have you noticed that the most efficient workman
is generally the busiest?

The patient who insists on diagnosing his own case
for the doctor usually needs a mental specialist.

It is easier to keep ahead
than to try to catch up with back work.

Laziness usually is nothing but a bad liver
and a clogged sewer system.

When the other fellow's facial expression looks pained it's
time to stop talking or change the conversation.

Where does the philosopher learn so much about the
mistakes men make? From those who make them!

The doctor's mental attitude is his main source of
protection against disease. And it is your, too.

Be careful with a hazardous job.
Death is very permanent!

It is better to earn a promotion than to gripe for it.

Keep your sewer system clean
and put the doctor's fee into war bonds.

Over-eating is costly. Both in grocer's bills and doctor's bills.

Your real boss is the one who walks around under your hat.

Never ask for anything you haven't earned in advance
and likely you'll never be turned down.

Every time you think in terms of benefit to your employer,
you come one step nearer an equal benefit for yourself.

The chances are that your job likes you precisely
as much as you like it, but no more.

Loafing on your job hurts your employer,
but it hurts you more.

Don't ask your employer why you are not promoted.
Ask the person who really knows best—yourself.

If you have more enemies than friends,
the odds are a thousand to one
you have earned them.

The best executive doesn't spend
all his time in a swivel chair.

You'll always be welcome if you bring a smile
with you and leave your worries at home.

If you could see an opportunity as quickly
as you see the faults of others, you'd soon be rich.

It doesn't pay to look at others
through a foggy mental attitude.

A good set of brakes is more important than a dependable
self-starter, for both men and automobiles.

Talking behind a man's back
never hurts provided you say the right thing.

An apology is a healthy indication that a man
still is on speaking terms with his own conscience.

Never tear down anything unless you are prepared
to build something better in its place.

Never call a braggart down;
he will do a much better job for himself.

Don't be too hard on the fellow who is always griping,
for he is making life pretty tough for himself as it is.

It takes more than a loud voice
to gain respect for authority.

Misfortune seldom tangles with the man whose constant body-guards are hope and faith.

—NAPOLEON HILL

An ignorant man is more to be pitied than condemned.

○————○

If you really do your best you probably will not
have to think up an alibi for not having done better.

○————○

Whine about your misfortunes
and thereby multiply them,
but keep still and starve them out.

○————○

Silence has one major advantage: it gives no one
a clue as to what your next move will be.

○————○

When you become so angry you don't know what to do,
it will be safer to do nothing.

Wisdom consists in knowing what not to want
as well as what to want.

It is a sure thing that you'll not finish if you don't start.

Never try to drive a sharp bargain with life
unless you are willing to take the worse of it.

No matter whom you cheat, nor of what you cheat him,
you cheat yourself more.

Isn't it going just a little too far to ask the creator to do
something for you which you could do for yourself?

A rudderless ship and a purposeless man
are eventually stranded on a desert sand.

Time is a relentless master.
It forces everything to gravitate
to where it belongs by its nature.

The eternal Law of Compensation balances everything
throughout the universe with its opposite of an equal force.

If you must gripe, why not gripe for a bigger
opportunity to be useful to others?

A good football team consists in harmonious coordination
of effort more than in individual skill.

When you count your winnings after an argument
with your boss, don't forget to deduct your losses, too.

Riches without gratitude are apt to become liabilities.

Where will you be and what will you be
ten years from now if you keep on
the way you are going?

A man's progress in life begins in his own mind
and ends the same place.

Keep so busy going after what you want that you have no
time to fear what you don't want.

Your big pay off comes at the end of the second mile.

The only safe way to boast is by
constructive deeds and not words.

Plain stubbornness if often mistaken for "pride."

You probably never heard of a professional gambler
who made a fortune and kept it.

If you have no major purpose
you are drifting toward certain failure.

A poor loser nearly always is on the losing side.

Don't take a man too seriously when he says "come and
see me sometime." Seriousness is generally specific.

Loud threats often indicate deep fears.

The most biting pain comes from a sharp tongue.

Remember that disagreements seldom are one-sided.

The successful person has learned that "whatever the mind of man can conceive and believe the mind of man can achieve." And this person keeps on keeping on until he converts his stumbling blocks into stepping stones. He knows that with every adversity comes the seed of an equivalent benefit.

−NAPOLEON HILL

Printed in the USA
CPSIA information can be obtained
at www.ICGtesting.com
JSHW012038140824
68134JS00033B/3140